San Diego
Travel Guide

Quick Trips Series

No part of this publication may be reproduced, stored in a retrieval system, or transmitted, in any form or by any means without the prior written permission of the publisher, nor be otherwise circulated in any form of binding or cover other than that in which it is published and without similar condition being imposed on the subsequent purchaser. If there are any errors or omissions in copyright acknowledgements the publisher will be pleased to insert the appropriate acknowledgement in any subsequent printing of this publication. Although we have taken all reasonable care in researching this book we make no warranty about the accuracy or completeness of its content and disclaim all liability arising from its use.

Copyright © 2016, Astute Press
All Rights Reserved.

Table of Contents

SAN DIEGO — 6
- CUSTOMS & CULTURE 7
- GEOGRAPHY 9
- WEATHER & BEST TIME TO VISIT 9

SIGHTS & ACTIVITIES: WHAT TO SEE & DO — 12
- AMUSEMENT ATTRACTIONS & ZOOS 12
  - Legoland California 13
  - San Diego Zoo 14
  - San Diego Zoo Safari Park 15
  - SeaWorld San Diego 16
- BEACHES 17
  - Mission Beach 18
  - Sunset Cliffs Beach 19
  - Coronado Dog Beach 20
  - Ocean Beach 21
- HIKING & OTHER ACTIVITIES 21
  - One Father Junipero Serra Trail 22
  - Seaforth Boat Rental 22
  - San Diego Chargers 23
  - San Diego Padres 24
  - Oceanside Beaches 25
- MISSIONS & MUSEUMS 26
  - San Diego de Alcala (California's First Mission) 27
  - USS Midway Museum 28
  - Historic Gaslamp Quarter 29
- PARKS & NATURAL GARDENS 30

Balboa Park 31
Cabrillo National Monument 31
Living Coast Discovery Center 32
Botanic Gardens 33

BUDGET TIPS 35

🌐 ACCOMMODATION 35

Hard Rock Hotel San Diego 36
Ocean Beach Cottages 37
Holiday Inn San Diego on the Bay 38
Dolphin Motel 39
Howard Johnson Inn SeaWorld 40

🌐 RESTAURANTS, CAFÉS & BARS 41

Harbor House Restaurant 42
The Trails Eatery 43
Café 56 44
California Pizza Kitchen 45
OB Noodle House 46

🌐 SHOPPING 47

Old Towne San Diego 48
Seaport Village 48
Horton Plaza 49
Las Americas Premium Outlets 50
Captain's Cove 50

KNOW BEFORE YOU GO 52

🌐 ENTRY REQUIREMENTS 52

🌐 HEALTH INSURANCE 53

🌐 TRAVELING WITH PETS 54

🌐 AIRPORTS 56

🌐 AIRLINES 60

🌐 HUBS 63

🌐 SEAPORTS 65

- Money Matters 67
- Currency 67
- Banking/ATMs 67
- Credit Cards 68
- Tourist Tax 69
- Sales Tax 70
- Tipping 71
- Connectivity 72
- Mobile Phones 72
- Dialing Code 74
- Emergency Numbers 74
- General Information 74
- Public Holidays 74
- Time Zones 75
- Daylight Savings Time 77
- School Holidays 77
- Trading Hours 78
- Driving 78
- Drinking 80
- Smoking 81
- Electricity 82
- Food & Drink 83
- American Sports 85
- Useful Websites 87

SAN DIEGO TRAVEL GUIDE

San Diego

San Diego is one of North America's most appealing cities and is located on the Pacific Ocean in Southern California. The city has beautiful beaches, a warm climate, top universities, famous biotech and hi-tech companies, a great nightlife, an outdoor culture and well-established ethnic diversity. San Diego is conveniently

SAN DIEGO TRAVEL GUIDE

located close to Orange County and Los Angeles and is just north of Tijuana, Mexico.

With a population of 1.4 million, it is the second-largest city in California. Despite being a major city, San Diego is relatively slow-paced and is a good choice for a city break by the beach. Whether you're looking for a family trip or a couple's getaway you will love your time in beautiful San Diego.

Sun chasers will enjoy the 70 miles of pristine beaches. The beaches are as diverse as the visitors to the area. You'll find a spot in the sand suitable for families, dogs, or the sports enthusiast and with reliable weather very few days at the beach are spoiled by rain or cold in San Diego!

SAN DIEGO TRAVEL GUIDE

With historical sites, museums, amusement parks, zoos, and a hip, casual downtown dining and shopping scene, San Diego has something for everyone.

🌐 Customs & Culture

San Diego attracts vacationers and residents from other parts of the United States and Mexico. With its prosperity, stable economy, and attractions, San Diego sees an influx of people most years.

San Diegans are known for being relaxed, casual, and courteous. The people of San Diego make visitors feel welcome, comfortable, and safe.

If you want to blend in with the locals, wear casual clothing and use layers a part of your attire to accommodate the cooler mornings and late night breezes.

SAN DIEGO TRAVEL GUIDE

San Diego is a city in high-demand and visiting can be expensive. Locals who live in the city are accustomed to higher costs (i.e. rents, mortgages, insurance, food, and gas). Nevertheless, it is possible to visit San Diego inexpensively if you are careful.

You will find many educated people in San Diego, as it is home to several universities and colleges. Also, sports are a large part of the San Diegan culture with its pro-football and baseball teams.

🌐 Geography

San Diego is in a prime location in the United States. About 120 miles south of Los Angeles, San Diego is snuggled among the Laguna Mountains on the east and the Pacific Coast on the west, with over 200 hills and

SAN DIEGO TRAVEL GUIDE

canyons dividing the mesas in between. Approximately 20 miles north of Mexico, San Diego is a gateway to Mexico.

🌐 Weather & Best Time to Visit

San Diego is known for its mild, temperate climate and you rarely see a bad weather day. You can count on sunny skies and warm breezes most of the year, making this a favorite destination for outdoor weddings!

Some people do plan around the "June gloom" and even, the "May gray." These times aren't the prettiest for San Diego or southern California. Because most people want to plan their vacations with optimal weather, you might find mid-to-late spring and early fall as more suitable.

SAN DIEGO TRAVEL GUIDE

April in San Diego has nice, warm days and sunny skies; while fall in San Diego, particularly late September and October, has the warmest days of the year as a result of hot, desert, Santa Ana winds that blow in.

Some people like to vacation and have a nice 'winter' in San Diego. You might find some locals shivering in Ugg boots and jackets, but many visitors to San Diego in the wintertime will enjoy the 60° F/16° C temperatures in their T-shirts and shorts!

Your trip might be best planned around your favorite interests. For surfing fans, fall and winter are your best bets to find waves with optimal swells and less crowded beaches.

SAN DIEGO TRAVEL GUIDE

Some amusement parks have amended times during certain parts of the year and a few have blackout dates. San Diego hosts several festivals throughout the year so schedule your vacation accordingly.

Don't forget the professional sporting events that San Diego offers. Football and baseball fans will enjoy tickets to a game or two.

SAN DIEGO TRAVEL GUIDE

Sights & Activities: What to See & Do

🌎 Amusement Attractions & Zoos

With Legoland California, San Diego Zoo Safari Park, San Diego Zoo, and SeaWorld San Diego, there is plenty of fun to be had! There is so much to do in San Diego that a person might not know where to begin or how to choose! Depending on your length of stay and budget, not to

SAN DIEGO TRAVEL GUIDE

mention your tired feet, you will want to be selective with the many theme park-like attractions of San Diego.

It is suggested that you consider your options with your holiday cohorts and choose one or two of these areas to attend per vacation. However, if you are gung-ho and ready to tackle more, there are coupon options or purchase "cards" that provide maximum participation in multiple park destinations. Likewise, prices are subject to change year to year so it is best to call ahead or check out websites for the most current fees.

Legoland California

1 Legoland Dr,

Carlsbad, CA 920008

(760) 918-5346

http://california.legoland.com/

SAN DIEGO TRAVEL GUIDE

Legoland California is the sight to see, bar none! With over 60 kid friendly rides, your group will love this, particularly, if it consists of the under twelves. Because Legoland California has no rides with height restrictions, people of all ages and sizes can take part in everything. With all the various exhibits made of legos, you will find yourself constantly amazed and asking "how do they do it?" Adults and children alike are awed by Miniland USA, consisting of popular and historic US sites constructed entirely out of legos!

Legoland California works hard to make sure its visitors feel welcome. Backpacks are permitted, as well as bringing water bottles and foods for people with special dietary needs. As with most places involving outdoors in southern California, you will want to have sunscreen and

SAN DIEGO TRAVEL GUIDE

a hat anytime of the year. There is also water fun at Legoland California, so it is best to wear clothes you're fine with getting wet or be prepared to skip that section.

San Diego Zoo

2920 Zoo Drive,

San Diego, CA 92101

(619) 231-1515

www.sandiegozoo.org/

World-renowned for its plethora of animals and spectacular design, the San Diego Zoo shouldn't be missed by any zoo aficionados. Located at Balboa Park of San Diego, it is distinguished as one of the largest zoos in the world! Home to over 4,000 animals, there is something for just about anyone. Whether you want to view the big cats, stalking gorillas, or yes, the famous pandas, the San Diego Zoo won't disappoint. The San Diego Zoo is accessible for all with its gondola skylifts and tour bus to support, however, it is strongly suggested that you plan out your visit wisely or schedule multiple days, as this place is definitely a large geographical undertaking!

San Diego Zoo Safari Park

15500 San Pasqual Valley Rd.

Escondido, CA 92027

http://www.sdzsafaripark.org/

The San Diego Zoo Safari Park is not just another zoo! It puts you in sight of a vast array of wild animals in their natural setting. You can have the feel of a real African Safari as you explore the multiple walking trails without ever leaving the continent! The Safari Park has all that

SAN DIEGO TRAVEL GUIDE

you expect: lions, cheetahs, elephants, gorillas, zebras, and much more. They even offer a chance of up close encounters with their safari tram tours, too, in addition to sky viewing with hot-air balloon rides. No matter what, you certainly won't want to miss the amazing and educational animal shows featuring birds and other rare and exotic animals!

Keep in mind that the Zoo Safari Park is not at the same locale as the San Diego Zoo. The Safari Park is approximately 30 miles north of the San Diego Zoo.

SeaWorld San Diego

500 SeaWorld Drive, San Diego, CA 92100

(619) 226-3901

seaworldparks.com/en/seaworld-sandiego/

SAN DIEGO TRAVEL GUIDE

SeaWorld San Diego has bragging rights as it was the original SeaWorld. There are now two others, one in San Antonio and the other in Orlando, but if you get the chance to visit just one, SeaWorld San Diego is it!

SeaWorld San Diego is a zoo/aquarium and amusement park with rides. With turtles, sharks, dolphins, penguins, beloved whales and Shamu, SeaWorld San Diego is top-notch for animal shows and exhibits. However, it also entices the thrill seekers with six sea-themed and adventure worthy rides! All of this makes SeaWorld San Diego a true contender among choices.

🌎 Beaches

With its warm weather, rare rain, and nearly 70 miles of sandy beaches, it is no wonder that vacationers to San Diego put beaches at the top of their must-do list. San

SAN DIEGO TRAVEL GUIDE

Diego has several beaches that are noteworthy candidates for holiday-makers; you just have to know which one suits your needs best. Are you looking for the quintessential California beach? Maybe you want that sleepy beach feel? Here are some of the best options for beaches San Diego has to offer!

Mission Beach

W. Mission Bay Drive at Ocean Front Walk

San Diego, CA 92109

http://www.sandiego.gov/lifeguards/beaches/mb.shtml

Mission Beach is the beach to head to if you're vacationing with family, especially little ones! It is clean, safe, has parking (though, that fills up quickly so you might end up parking along streets a little farther away than desired), restrooms, great views, and friendly people.

SAN DIEGO TRAVEL GUIDE

It is usually crowded in pique times (read: Summer), but there's always room for more. Honestly, if you can only visit one beach and you're looking for family friendly, look no further!

Some tips: Mission Beach has a boardwalk where lots of people skateboard, roller blade, bike, walk, and people watch. There are usually some tours and rental spots too, if you're interested. Bring your gear or just comfy shoes and take advantage of this. It will make your beach trip all the more memorable.

Sunset Cliffs Beach

1253 Sunset Cliffs Blvd

San Diego, CA 92107

Neighborhood: Ocean Beach

SAN DIEGO TRAVEL GUIDE

http://www.sandiego.gov/park-and-recreation/parks/shoreline/sunset.shtml

This is a hidden gem in San Diego among the beaches. It's rocky and has one of the most awesome views of the Pacific. This is where the San Diegans take their out-of-town guests for good views and nice walks! You'll need to pack shoes for the terrain, but there are plenty of areas for sitting and meditating on the beautiful surroundings! Note, since this isn't a typical beach park place, you won't find restrooms or snack stands. There is, however, a Jack in the Box fast food restaurant nearby that most find convenient enough if the need arises. By the way, it is said that at the hotel across the street, the television series, Veronica Mars, was filmed.

SAN DIEGO TRAVEL GUIDE

Coronado Dog Beach

100 Ocean Blvd

Coronado, CA 92118

Neighborhood: Coronado, San Diego County

(619) 522-7342

This beach is bound to please dog lovers and their best friends. You'll find lots of clean sand, ample residential parking along the streets nearby (there is beach parking, but that usually goes fast), and friendly people. It's 'bring your own poo bags' however, if you forget, there are always plenty around to share. This dog beach is still for human 'beach fun' too, so don't forget your boogie board, sunscreen, and beach umbrella. People come to relax and stay all day. The vibe is definitely California style and you and your pet are sure to enjoy the atmosphere.

SAN DIEGO TRAVEL GUIDE

Ocean Beach

1950 Abbott St

San Diego, CA 92107

Neighborhood: Ocean Beach and Point Loma

http://www.sandiego.gov/lifeguards/beaches/ob.shtml

This beach is known as a hip, diverse spot to the locals. It is not what you might think of as the cleanest beach, nor is it considered a family-focused beach. But, if you are looking for something different and atypical on your beach visit, then this is the beach for you. It has locally owned establishments all around, which translates to plenty of interesting stores for shopping and eating. Definitely if you feel like an afternoon of people watching and some cool waves, give Ocean Beach a try!

SAN DIEGO TRAVEL GUIDE

🌍 Hiking & Other Activities

With beaches, mountains, and professional teams, San Diego is a haven for active and sports-minded people. In addition to your beach fun or in lieu of, San Diego offers several places for hiking, biking and trail walking; boating and kayaking; and sports watching of several pro teams.

One Father Junipero Serra Trail

San Diego, CA 92119-1008

(619)405-0177

http://www.mtrp.org/

If you can only do one hike then this is the place to do it! With 42 miles of trails, free guided tours, a large visitor center, nearby lakes, and only 12 miles from downtown San Diego, it is unbeatable. A favorite of locals with its year round schedule and frequent events, but also

SAN DIEGO TRAVEL GUIDE

equipped for tourists having souvenir shops and guided tours, One Father Junipero Serra is fun for families, couples, individuals, and also known to be pet friendly!

Seaforth Boat Rental

1641 Quivera Rd, San Diego, CA 92109

(888) 834-BOAT (Toll-Free)

(619) 223-1681

http://www.seaforthboatrental.com/

Sometimes, the only way to do it right, is to do it up close and personal! That's what you get with Seaforth Boat Rentals, located in the Mission Beach area. If you want to add on to your beach day, or take your beach day a little closer to the ocean, then renting kayaks, boats, or jet skis might be for you. Seaforth has tour options, with expert guides; or if you want, you can rent and explore on your own the intricacies of the Pacific, the San Diegan way.

Seaforth is prepared for the beginners, as well as the seasoned renters. They have everything you need and their professional staff is ready to help you with any questions. With the myriad of options, you can definitely find something to fit your time and budget!

San Diego Chargers

Qualcomm Stadium

9449 Friars Rd

San Diego, CA

(619) 281-6316

http://www.chargers.com/

SAN DIEGO TRAVEL GUIDE

San Diego Padres

Petco Park

19 Tony Gwynn Way

San Diego, CA 92101

(619) 795-5000

http://sandiego.padres.mlb.com/index.jsp?c_id=sd&sv=1

You might find that your holiday coincides with the professional sports teams of San Diego, whether it is the San Diego Chargers of the NFL, or the San Diego baseball team, the Padres. If so, you won't regret attending a game, sitting in the stadium, and cheering on the team like a San Diegan, or rooting for your own visiting team if it so happens. Even those that are not football or baseball devotees can't help but catch the contagious fever from the enthusiastic crowd.

SAN DIEGO TRAVEL GUIDE

Definitely consider adding this to your vacation if the schedule permits it. You can find tickets that fit any budget, if you aren't afraid of heights!

Oceanside Beaches

200 N the Strand, Oceanside, CA 92054

(619) 281-6316

http://www.sandiego.org/what-to-do/beaches/oceanside.aspx

Finally, surfing is the classic California sport and might be just what you're looking for to wrap up your vacation adventures. You will find most California beaches have surfers and/or offer surfing themed shops, restaurants, or gear; it is all part of the culture. To narrow down the overwhelming surfing spots, try Oceanside Harbor, also

SAN DIEGO TRAVEL GUIDE

known as "The Jetties", or Oceanside City Beach, called "The Strand."

These areas are really focused on the experienced surfer, but they're excellent for newcomers, too. You'll find a mixture of parking (i.e. street, lots, and metered), which means there will be something available, just perhaps not your first choice. The City Beach, a.k.a. The Strand, also has showers to rinse off after and plenty of restrooms. Although the beaches are popular for surfers, you'll still find swimmers and families, too, so this might make the area even more attractive for you.

A few things to remember: Have change for the meter (it might turn out to be your best parking choice) and plan to visit the California Surf Museum. The museum alone puts the Oceanside Beaches ahead of the others!

SAN DIEGO TRAVEL GUIDE

🌐 Missions & Museums

Don't forget about San Diego's rich and diverse history! From missions to museums, your vacation can be educational, too. A nice note to remember is that most of these are inexpensive in comparison to other attractions, if not completely free.

San Diego de Alcala (California's First Mission)

10818 San Diego Mission Rd.

San Diego, CA 92108-2429

(619) 281-8449

http://parks.ca.gov/?page_id=22722

Historically, California is known for its missions as much as its beaches! Hundreds of years ago, Europeans explored California, particularly the Spanish, and used

SAN DIEGO TRAVEL GUIDE

missions as ways to ingrain themselves with the natives. Missions provided protection for European explorers and settlers, and a means to religiously and politically indoctrinate. Now, missions represent the rich history of western United States, albeit at times darkened by strife. If you have the chance, you will want to see these up close.

You can take the famous California Missions Trails along Interstate 5 to Highway 101 and drive the sites of the missions from San Diego north, past Los Angeles, to Sonoma. You'll see 21 missions this way! However, if you prefer to get up close and personal and not leave San Diego, take time to visit the site of where it all began 243 years ago at San Diego Mission Road, the home of California's first mission.

SAN DIEGO TRAVEL GUIDE

USS Midway Museum

910 N. Harbor Drive

San Diego, CA 92101

(619) 544-9600

http://www.tripadvisor.com/Travel-g60750-d531819/San-Diego:California:Uss.Midway.Museum.html

San Diego has a multitude of museums, but if you have to be selective, this is a sure winner! The ship, located off a pier close to downtown and accessible by Trolley, is a true, navy aircraft carrier and was active for 47 years. Still containing real planes and jets, you can feel free to touch and get hands-on with it all. Sit in the planes, walk through the kitchens, and explore the whole boat! Kids of all ages will enjoy living history and certainly adults are as engaged as the youngsters.

SAN DIEGO TRAVEL GUIDE

Some things to consider if you want to make this part of your holiday: Expect to spend at least three hours, even on a self-guided tour, if you want to experience it all; be prepared for lots of walking up and down stairs and in tight quarters at times; and, it is said that the Captain's bridge gets crowded quickly so you might want to put it first on your list to see. There is a fee for the museum so check ahead if you are concerned about pricing, as fees are subject to change from year to year.

Historic Gaslamp Quarter

614 5th Avenue. Ste E

San Diego, CA 92101

(619) 233-5227

http://www.gaslamp.org/

SAN DIEGO TRAVEL GUIDE

This is where the city of San Diego all began. The historic Gaslamp Quarter looks like a conglomeration of shops, businesses, restaurants, entertainment and such, but that's like saying there is nothing more than that in the French Quarter of New Orleans! Don't be swayed by the shopping and dining; there's plenty of time for that later! However, take your time walking the Gaslamp Quarter to view the characteristic, Victorian homes and other historical architecture. You'll be glad you did.

There is a convenient Trolley system that can take you from just about anywhere in the San Diego area to the Gaslamp Quarter; there is even a route from the Mexican border to the Gaslamp Quarter!

SAN DIEGO TRAVEL GUIDE

🌐 Parks & Natural Gardens

San Diego also offers parks and natural gardens suited for those wanting less commercial effect and instead, more of a quieter, peaceful vibe for their holiday. You'll find these locales give you a real sense of the flora and fauna of San Diego.

Balboa Park

1549 El Prado

San Diego, CA 92101

(619) 239-0512

http://www.balboapark.org/

Now Balboa Park is one of the most famous parks in the country and houses many of the other attractions that you may be considering, for example, the San Diego Zoo. However, with over 1200 acres, it also contains so many other attractions and exhibits that it is worth mentioning on its own. Keep in mind that the sheer size of this 'park' makes it impossible to see everything, even if you dedicated your entire holiday. Nevertheless, a day spent here is not misplaced. With fifteen major museums, lush gardens, performing arts and theaters, and even an outside carousel, you will find more than you can handle.

Cabrillo National Monument

San Diego, CA

(619) 557-5450

http://www.nps.gov/cabr/index.htm

Set on 144 acres, this exquisite monument and lighthouse has the most breathtaking views. You can view Mexico, downtown San Diego, and Coronado Island. This tribute

SAN DIEGO TRAVEL GUIDE

to Juan Cabrillo's exploration of the west coast is another San Diegan treasure fit for anyone.

Currently, there is a $5 per car entrance fee, but judging by the visitors there, no one is sorry for paying the nominal fee. It is best to plan at minimum a half day for this visit, but well worth it for those who enjoy views and history! Keep in mind that fees are subject to change from year to year so you should always check ahead to have the most recent information before setting out on your destination.

Living Coast Discovery Center

1000 Gunpowder Point Drive, Chula Vista, CA 91910

(619) 409-5900

http://www.thelivingcoast.org/

SAN DIEGO TRAVEL GUIDE

The Living Coast Discovery Center is a nonprofit zoo and aquarium. However, it's placed here because of its focus on preservation and conservation. It is a model of natural habitats. They welcome visitors to learn about their efforts to conserve and protect nature's creatures and lands.

Located on the San Diego Bay, they offer individual visits, group tours, classes and other events. It is certainly a contrast to the large zoos and aquariums of San Diego, but a treasure all of its own! The Living Coast Discovery Center has several pricing charts, depending on the size of your group and your ticket preferences; therefore, you should be prepared to check with them by phone or internet to know what to expect fee-wise.

SAN DIEGO TRAVEL GUIDE

Botanic Gardens

1230 Quail Gardens Drive

Encinitas, CA 92024

(760) 436-3036

http://www.sdbgarden.org/contact.htm

With 4 miles of trails and over 37 acres, the SD Botanic Gardens is a haven for plants and flowers. As well, it recently opened the largest hands-on children's garden on the west coast. You can explore trails, walk among various species of cultivated beauties, or take any number of classes. There are regularly sponsored events at the Botanic Gardens that many find enjoyable too.

It is located north of San Diego, about a 30 minute drive. In addition, there is an entrance and parking fee. Prices

SAN DIEGO TRAVEL GUIDE

are subject to change year to year so it is best to call ahead or check out their website for the most current charges before heading out.

SAN DIEGO TRAVEL GUIDE

Budget Tips

🌎 Accommodation

Because San Diego is such a popular destination for vacationers all year long, it has numerous options for places to stay. From downtown or the Gaslamp Quarter to the beaches or somewhere suburban, the choices can be overwhelming. No matter where you decide, there are a number of clean, affordable, and safe accommodations in San Diego that can help ensure your holiday is up to par. The following are several highly recommended hotels in some of the most popular San Diego areas that are sure to please and remain easy on the wallet!

Hard Rock Hotel San Diego

207 5th Avenue

San Diego, CA 92101

(877) 205-9319

http://www.hardrockhotelsd.com/

$150-$250/ night

This hotel is great for individuals, couples, or groups of adults who desire to stay in the center of the Gaslamp Quarter and close to downtown San Diego. It is hip, fun, and lively. Close to all the downtown hotspots, it is suited for those looking for excitement on their stay. It is mid-priced and won't break the budget, yet it offers all the

SAN DIEGO TRAVEL GUIDE

upgraded amenities that make a hotel stay feel special if you choose to splurge a time or two (i.e. using the mini bar, turn down service, spa, massage, night club and restaurant...).

Ocean Beach Cottages

5065 Brighton Avenue, San Diego, CA 92107

(877) 205-9319

http://www.travelpod.com/motel/Ocean_Beach_Cottages-San_Diego.html

$75- $150/night

This is true beach living in San Diego – come and meet the shabby chic! Staying here, you will feel like a real beach native.

SAN DIEGO TRAVEL GUIDE

A close walk to the beach, you'll smell the ocean's salty air day and evening. This is the best place to be for a quiet stay, or if you plan to take your family and want to enjoy the beach multiple days on a budget. Some cottages are equipped with barbeques and bikes-just ask. But, all have the basic amenities of home, with your cooking supplies and beach-style furnishings included. This would be a great place to start a beach-stay tradition if you plan to come back to San Diego year after year.

Holiday Inn San Diego on the Bay

1355 North Harbor Drive

San Diego, CA 92101

(619) 232-3861

http://www.holidayinn.com/hotels/us/en/san-diego/sanem/hoteldetail

SAN DIEGO TRAVEL GUIDE

$75-$150/night

This hotel is a great, family friendly choice. The chain is known around the world for catering to family needs, with in-room video gaming machines, casual dining that permits kids eating free, and swimming recreation. This particular hotel also features room service, concierge, indoor and outdoor pools, complimentary wireless internet, on-site laundry, among many other features.

Another downtown option, the Holiday Inn San Diego On the Bay is close to most all recommended sightseeing attractions. It is also a great option if you need airport shuttle, as it offers it at no charge several times throughout the day.

SAN DIEGO TRAVEL GUIDE

Dolphin Motel

2912 Garrison Street

San Diego, CA 92106

http://www.tripadvisor.com/Hotel_Review-g60750-d119769-Reviews-Dolphin_Motel-San_Diego_California.html

$55-$75/ per night

Just one block from the San Diego Harbor in the Point Loma area, this motel might first seem unappealing. However, reviews of past vacationers show that many of them are repeats to the motel and their comments will certainly change your mind. It is small and no-frills; that's at once obvious. Yet, it is also clean, safe, convenient, and has a reputation for going the extra mile with friendliness and service. They offer hair dryers, ironing

SAN DIEGO TRAVEL GUIDE

boards, ability to print your air boarding passes, and even use of a laptop! Although not advertised, they've even provided breakfast and snacks to guests on past visits. If you are looking to save money, want to be near the water, and aren't keen on luxury accommodations, you will find that this unassuming gem is just right for you!

Howard Johnson Inn SeaWorld

3330 Rosecrans Street

San Diego, CA 92110

http://howardjohnsonsandiego.com/

$55-$85/per night

Just two miles from SeaWorld and the beach and only four miles from downtown San Diego, the Howard Johnson is a great option. If you plan SeaWorld as part of your vacation, this is absolutely your best deal.

SAN DIEGO TRAVEL GUIDE

The Howard Johnson has a family-friendly reputation, and though it has never been recognized as a choice for luxury, with an average 4.0 star rating out of 5.0 on Expedia.com, you can trust that your stay will be comfortable and not disappointing.

🌎 Restaurants, Cafés & Bars

Like Los Angeles, San Diego is now host to a slew of food trucks (i.e. vendors serving from trucks alongside populated roadways). Local residents have their favorites and have come to accept these just like any other eating establishment. However, vacationers are sure to find them intriguing. If you happen by one, go ahead and try a taco or burrito, or whatever specialty might be offered. Most have delicious selections at exceptional prices. Nevertheless, San Diego has a smorgasbord of eateries,

SAN DIEGO TRAVEL GUIDE

from fine dining to fast food and all in between. Naturally, sea food and Mexican styles are abundant, but you'll find plenty other options too. Here are some of the most highly recommended restaurants in San Diego.

Harbor House Restaurant

831 West Harbor Drive

San Diego, CA 92101

(619) 232-1141

http://www.harborhousesd.com/

$10-$30

Harbor House is probably the most expensive restaurant recommended here, and still be considered budget conscious. However, it is a real San Diego treat and worth the slight splurge! Known for its seafood specialties, you will want to try one or more of the oyster, crab, or shrimp dishes.

It's casual dining with awesome harbor views. Certainly when you go, you'll want to sit out deck to really take it all in! Tip: Go at lunch time to get the lunch specials, which are quite a bit cheaper, but still offer plenty enough to eat!

The Trails Eatery

7389 Jackson Drive

San Diego, CA 92119

(619) 667-2233

http://thetrailseatery.com/

Under $10

A real neighborhood establishment, this place is local

SAN DIEGO TRAVEL GUIDE

owned and operated. It specializes in natural and organic foods, and even gluten-free whenever possible.

The food is fresh and visually pleasing with a wide array of sandwiches, burgers, and salads, but the real prize is their breakfasts, served all day.

Don't waste time on the other stuff; once you feast your eyes on the cinnamon roll pancakes, Eggs Benedicts, and waffle selections from the menu, you'll have trouble deciding on just one breakfast!

On a side note, The Trails Eatery was featured in 2011 on the television show, Restaurant Impossible, with Robert Irvine. Despite excellent food ratings, this humble eatery suffered from some mismanagement and bad business decisions, which made it eligible for some heroic support from Mr. Irvine and his magical team. It is now on the upswing and the food is as good as ever!

Café 56

13211 Black Mountain Road

San Diego, CA 92129

(858) 484-5789

http://www.sandiegohomecooking.com/

$11- $30

Located in the neighborhood of Ranchos Penasquitos in San Diego, this is home cooking not to miss! Moderately priced, Café 56 serves breakfast, lunch, and dinner, but the raves are really all about the breakfast. They have all the breakfast home-cooking favorites, but also the Fiestas, too! You can find traditional, Mexican fare here to please.

SAN DIEGO TRAVEL GUIDE

Learn from the insider. If you have your dogs with you on your vacation, feel free to bring them here and eat on the patio. Café 56 will serve your pets fresh water from their water bowls and the waitresses and waiters are known to bring them a snack or two as well!

California Pizza Kitchen

11602 Carmel Mountain Road, San Diego, CA 92128

(858)675-4424

http://www.cpk.com/

$11- $30

Now, for many, the CPK would never make a recommendation list for the sheer factor of it being a popular, chain restaurant.

SAN DIEGO TRAVEL GUIDE

However, it makes this list for several reasons. First and foremost, it has good, quality food that you can count on for freshness and consistency. Second, if you are vacationing, you might not be familiar with the CPK; thus, it becomes a 'California novelty.' Third and last, it has a menu that can be easily be adjusted to fit any budget. Sure you can indulge and order appetizers, large entrees, dessert, and wine. But, you can find more than enough choices to satisfy for your hunger without making a large dent in your pocketbook, too.

As well, the CPK's atmosphere, staff, and menu make even the pickiest child eater, hippest college crowd, and most discerning, older couple feel at home.

SAN DIEGO TRAVEL GUIDE

OB Noodle House

2218 Cable Street

San Diego, CA 92107

(619)450-6868

http://www.obnoodlehouse.com/

Under $10

It might seem like Vietnamese noodles aren't typical for beach eateries, but remember, San Diego is anything but typical! If you are in the mood for good, warm noodles swimming in a tastefully seasoned broth, you must try OB Noodle House! Over 641 Yelp reviewers have rated OB Noodle House and it comes out with 4.0 stars out of 5.0 possible! And, at these prices, less than $10, what is there to lose?

SAN DIEGO TRAVEL GUIDE

Just be aware, the place is small and popular, meaning you will surely have a wait. In fact, you might plan to take yours to go or eat outside. OB Noodle House is also known for specials on drinks!

🌎 Shopping

Whether you're staying in downtown San Diego or at the beach, there is plenty of shopping to go around. Of course, you will find that all the attractions have their own gift shops and souvenirs from which to purchase mementos of your trip. Your hotel might even have its own shop, too. Without a doubt, there is a plethora of shopping establishments in San Diego and here are just a few budget saving places that are highly recommended.

SAN DIEGO TRAVEL GUIDE

Old Towne San Diego

2415 San Diego Avenue, Suite 107

San Diego, CA 92110

(619) 291-4903

http://www.oldtownsandiegoguide.com/index.html

http://www.oldtownsandiego.org/

Here you can experience shopping that caters to the birthplace of San Diego. You'll find shopping that fits every budget and interest. Candles, candy, leather, books, clothing and much more are the focuses of the various specialty shops available. Shopping fans can easily wile away an entire day and still not have experienced all that's offered!

SAN DIEGO TRAVEL GUIDE

Seaport Village

849 West Harbor Drive, #D

San Diego, CA 92101

(619) 235-4014

http://www.seaportvillage.com/

This place is a tourist's dream! Having over 50 shops, this is a sea paradise of souvenirs, trinkets, beach items, clothes, and more. It is designed to keep you happy all day, with its outdoor carousel, marina, and lagoon, as well as the 17+ eateries.

Horton Plaza

3958 5th Avenue

San Diego, CA 92101

(619) 220-6802

http://www.westfield.com/hortonplaza/

SAN DIEGO TRAVEL GUIDE

This is the mall, San Diego style. With its outdoor walkways, paths, and trails leading to and from shops, in addition to indoor areas, this place is more European Villa than shopping mall! It contains all the staples of malls across America like Macy's and Nordstrom's (pricey, but their clearance racks are notorious for great bargains!), a large movie theater, and snack/restaurant services. However, it also has some unique and independent shops. In actuality, you'll love the atmosphere as much as the shopping here. It is relaxing, vibrant, and sociable.

Las Americas Premium Outlets

4211 Camino de la Plaza

San Diego, CA 92173

(619) 934-8400

http://www.premiumoutlets.com/outlets/outlet.asp?id=76

SAN DIEGO TRAVEL GUIDE

This collection of high-end, name-brand outlet stores is just the thing for particular buyers who want to save money. In their 125 stores, you'll find your favorite items at reduced prices. Adidas, Guess, Tommy Hilfiger, J. Crew, and Coach are just a few. The San Diego Blue line Trolley makes this a no-hassle shopping experience.

Captain's Cove

851 West Harbor Drive

Downtown/Gaslamp, San Diego, CA 92101

(619) 234-5050

http://www.discoversd.com/shopping/captains-cove/2639.html

Located near the neighborhood of Little Italy, this is a quite unique gift and novelty shop, specializing is

SAN DIEGO TRAVEL GUIDE

seafaring items. From lighthouses to shells to clocks and ship bells, you are bound to find your treasure, not exactly hidden, in this popular, 30 year old Gaslamp shop. Some items might be a bit pricier than others, but the discerning shopper will find his or her bargain!

SAN DIEGO TRAVEL GUIDE

Know Before You Go

Entry Requirements

The Visa Waiver Programme (VWP) allows nationals of selected countries to enter the United States for tourism or certain types of business without requiring a visa. This applies to citizens of the UK, Australia, New Zealand, Canada, Chile, Denmark, Belgium, Austria, Latvia, Estonia, Finland, Italy, Hungary, Iceland, France, Germany, Japan, Spain, Portugal, Norway, Sweden, Slovenia, Slovakia, Switzerland, Brunei, Taiwan, South Korea, Luxemburg, Singapore, Liechtenstein, Monaco, Malta, San Marino, Lithuania, Greece, the Netherlands and the Czech Republic. To qualify, you will also need to have a passport with integrated chip, also known as an e-Passport. The e-Passport symbol has to be clearly displayed on the cover of the passport. This secure method of identification will protect and verify the holder in case of identity theft and other breaches of privacy. There are exceptions. Visitors with a criminal record, serious communicable illness or those who were deported or refused entry on a past occasion will not qualify for the Visa Waiver Program and will need to apply for a visa. Holders of a UK passport who have dual citizenship of Iraq, Iran, Sudan, Syria, Somalia, Libya or Yemen (or those who have travelled to the above countries after 2011) will also need to apply for a visa. A requirement of the Visa Waiver Programme is online registration with the Electronic System for Travel Authorisation (ESTA) at least 72 hours before your travels. When entering the United States, you will be able to skip the custom declaration and proceed directly to an Automated Passport Control (APC) kiosk.

If travelling from a non-qualifying country, you will need a visitor's visa, also known as a non-immigrant visa when entering the United States for visiting friends or family, tourism or medical procedures. It is recommended that you schedule your visa interview at least 60 days before your date of travel. You will need to submit a passport that will be valid for at least 6 months after your intended travel, a birth certificate, a police certificate and color photographs that comply with US visa requirements. Proof of financial support for your stay in the United States is also required.

Health Insurance

Medical procedures are very expensive in the United States and there is no free or subsidized healthcare service. The best strategy would be to organize temporary health insurance for the duration of your stay. You will not need any special vaccinations if visiting the United States as tourists. For an immigration visa, the required immunizations are against hepatitis A and B, measles, mumps, rubella, influenza, polio, tetanus, varicella, meningococcal, pneumococcal, rotavirus, pertussis and influenza type B.

There are several companies that offer short-term health insurance packages for visitors to the United States. Coverage with Inbound USA can be purchased online through their website and offer health insurance for periods from 5 to 364 days. Visitor Secure will provide coverage for accidents and new health complications from 5 days to 2 years, but the cost and care of pre-existing medical conditions and dental care is excluded. Inbound Guest offers similar terms for periods of between 5 and 180 days and will email you a virtual membership card as soon as the contract is finalized. Physical cards will be available within one business day of arrival to the United States.

Traveling with Pets

The United States accepts EU pet passports as valid documentation for pets in transit, provided that your pet is up to date on vaccinations. In most instances, the airline you use will require a health certificate. While microchipping is not required,

SAN DIEGO TRAVEL GUIDE

it may be helpful in case your pet gets lost. If visiting from a non-English speaking country, be sure to have an English translation of your vet's certificate available for the US authorities to examine. To be cleared for travel, your pet must have a vet's certificate issued no less than 10 days before your date of travel. Pets need to be vaccinated against rabies at least 30 days prior to entry to the United States. If the animal was recently microchipped, the microchipping procedure should have taken place prior to vaccination. In the case of dogs, it is also important that your pet must test negative for screwworm no later than 5 days before your intended arrival in the United States.

In the case of exotic pets such as parrots, turtles and other reptiles, you will need check on the CITES (Convention on International Trade in Endangered Species of Wild Fauna and Flora) status of the breed, to ensure that you will in fact be allowed to enter the United States with your pet. There are restrictions on bringing birds from certain countries and a quarantine period of 30 days also applies for birds, such as parrots. It is recommended that birds should enter the United States at New York, Los Angeles or Miami, where quarantine facilities are available. The owner of the bird will carry the expense of the quarantine and advance reservations need to be made for this, to prevent the bird being refused entry altogether. Additionally, you will need to submit documentation in the

SAN DIEGO TRAVEL GUIDE

form of a USDA import permit as well as a health certificate issued by your veterinarian less than 30 days prior to the date of entry.

Airports

Your trip will probably be via one of the country's major gateway airports. **Hartsfield–Jackson Atlanta International Airport** (ATL), which is located less than 12km from the central business area of Atlanta in Georgia is the busiest airport in the United States and the world. It processes about 100 million passengers annually. Internationally, it offers connections to Paris, London, Frankfurt Amsterdam, Dubai, Tokyo, Mexico City and Johannesburg. Domestically, its busiest routes are to Florida, New York, Los Angeles, Dallas and Chicago. Delta Airlines maintains a huge presence at the airport, with the largest hub to be found anywhere in the world and a schedule of almost a thousand daily flights. Via a railway station, the airport provides easy access to the city.

Los Angeles International Airport (LAX) is the second busiest airport in the United States and the largest airport in the state of California. Located in the southwestern part of Los Angeles about 24km from the city center, it is easily accessibly by road and rail. Its nine passenger terminals are connected

SAN DIEGO TRAVEL GUIDE

through a shuttle service. Los Angeles International Airport is a significant origin-and-destination airport for travellers to and from the United States. The second busiest airport in California is **San Francisco International Airport** (SFO) and, like Los Angeles it is an important gateway for trans-Pacific connections. It serves as an important maintenance hub for United and is home to an aviation museum. Anyone who is serious about green policies and environmentally friendly alternatives will love San Francisco's airport. There is a special bicycle route to the airport, designated bicycle parking zones and even a service that offers special freight units for travelling with your bicycle. Bicycles are also allowed on its Airtrain service. The third airport of note in California is **San Diego International Airport** (SAN).

Chicago O'Hare International Airport (ORD) is located about 27km northwest of Chicago's central business district, also known as the Chicago Loop. As a gateway to Chicago and the Great Lakes region, it is the US airport that sees the highest frequency of arrivals and departures. Terminal 5 is used for all international arrivals and most international departures, with the exception of Air Canada and some airline carriers under the Star Alliance or Oneworld brand. The Airport Transit System provides easy access for passengers between terminals and to the remote sections of the parking area.

SAN DIEGO TRAVEL GUIDE

Located roughly halfway between the cities of Dallas and Fort Worth, **Dallas-Fort Worth International Airport** (DFW) is the primary international airport serving the state of Texas. Both in terms of passenger numbers and air traffic statistics, it ranks among the ten busiest airports in the world. It is also home to the second largest hub in the world, that of American Airlines, which is headquartered in Texas. Through 8 Interstate highways and 3 major rail services, it provides access to the city centers of both Dallas and Fort Worth, as well as the rest of Texas. An automated people mover, known as the Skylink makes it effortless for passenger to transverse between different sections of the airport and the parking areas. Terminal D is its international terminal. The second busiest airport in Texas is the **George Bush Intercontinental Airport** (IAH) in Houston, which offers connections to destinations across the United States, as well as Mexico, Canada, the Americas and selected cities in Europe and Asia.

John F. Kennedy International Airport (JFK) is located in the neighborhood of Queens. In terms of international passengers, it is one of the busiest airports in the United States, with connections to 6 continents and with the air traffic of 70 different airlines. Its busiest routes are to London, Paris, Los Angeles and San Francisco. It serves as a gateway hub for both Delta and American Airlines. Terminal 8, its newest terminal, is larger than Central Park. It has the capacity of processing

SAN DIEGO TRAVEL GUIDE

around 1600 passengers per hour. An elevated railway service, the Airtrain provides access to all 8 of its terminals and also connects to the Long Island railroad as well as the New York City Subway in Queens. Within the airport, the service is free. Three other major airports also service the New York City area. **Newark Liberty International Airport** (EWR) is New York's second busiest airport and home of the world's third largest hub, that of United Airlines. Newark is located about 24km from Mid Manhattan, between Newark and Elizabeth. Its airtrain offers an easy way of commuting around the airport and connects via the Newark Liberty International Airport Station to the North Jersey Coast line and Northeast Corridor line. Other airports in New York are **La Guardia Airport** (LGA), located on the Flushing Bay Waterfront in Queens and **Teterboro Airport** (TEB), which is mainly used by private charter companies.

Washington D.C. is served by two airports, **Baltimore-Washington International Airport** (BWI) and **Washington Dulles International Airport** (IAD). Other important airports on the eastern side of the United States include **Logan International Airport** (BOS) in Boston, **Philadelphia International Airport** (PHL) and **Charlotte Douglas International Airport** (CLT) in North Carolina. The three busiest airports in the state of Florida are **Miami International Airport** (MIA), **Fort Lauderdale-Hollywood International**

SAN DIEGO TRAVEL GUIDE

Airport (FLL) and **Tampa International Airport** (TPA). In the western part of the United States, **McCarran International Airport** (LAS) in Las Vegas and **Phoenix Sky Harbor International** (PHX) in Arizona offer important connections. **Denver International Airport** (DEN) in Colorado is the primary entry point to Rocky Mountains, while **Seattle-Tacoma International Airport** (SEA) in Washington State and **Portland International Airport** (PDX) in Oregon provide access to the Pacific Northwest. **Honolulu International Airport** (HNL) is the primary point of entry to Hawaii.

Airlines

The largest air carriers in the United States are United Airlines, American Airlines and Delta Airlines. Each of these could lay claim to the title of largest airline using different criteria. In terms of passenger numbers, Delta Airlines is the largest airline carrier. It was founded from humble beginnings as a crop dusting outfit in the 1920s, but grew to an enormous operation through mergers with Northeast Airlines in the 1970s, Western Airlines in the 1980s and North-western Airlines in 2010. Delta also absorbed a portion of Pan Am's assets and business, following its bankruptcy in the early 1990s. Delta Airlines operates Delta Connections, a regional service covering North American destinations in Canada, Mexico and the United

SAN DIEGO TRAVEL GUIDE

States. In terms of destinations, United Airlines is the largest airline in the United States and the world. Its origins lie in an early airline created by Boeing in the 1920s, but the company grew from a series of acquisitions and mergers - most recently with Continental Airlines - to its current status as a leading airline. Regional services are operated under the brand United Express, in partnership with a range of feeder carriers including CapeAir, CommutAir, ExpressJet, GoJet Airlines, Mesa Airlines, Republic Airlines, Shuttle America, SkyWest Airlines and Trans State Airlines. American Airlines commands the largest fleet in the United States. It originated from the merger of over 80 tiny regional airlines in the 1930s and has subsequently merged with Trans Caribbean Airways, Air California, Reno Air, Trans World Airlines and, most recently, US Airways. Through the Oneworld Airline Alliance, American Airlines is partnered with British Airways, Finnair, Iberia and Japan Airlines. Regional connections are operated under the American Eagle brand name and include the services of Envoy Air, Piedmont Airlines, Air Wisconsin, SkyWest Airlines, Republic Airlines and PSA Airlines. American Airlines operates the American Airlines Shuttle, a service that connects the cities of New York, Boston and Washington DC with hourly flights on weekdays.

Based in Dallas, Texas, Southwest Airlines is the world's largest budget airline. It carries the highest number of domestic

SAN DIEGO TRAVEL GUIDE

passengers in the United States and operates over 200 daily flights on its 3 busiest routes, namely Chicago, Washington and Las Vegas. JetBlue Airways is a budget airline based in Long Island that operates mainly in the Americas and the Caribbean. It covers 97 destinations in the United States, Mexico, Costa Rica, Puerto Rico, Grenada, Peru, Colombia, Bermuda, Jamaica, the Bahamas, Barbados, the Dominican Republic and Trinidad and Tobago. Spirit Airlines is an ultra low cost carrier which offers flights to destinations in the United States, Latin America, Mexico and the Caribbean. It is based in Miramar, Florida.

Alaska Airlines was founded in the 1930s to offer connections in the Pacific Northwest, but began to expand from the 1990s to include destinations east of the Rocky Mountains as well as connections to the extreme eastern part of Russia. Alaska Airlines recently acquired the brand, Virgin America which represents the Virgin brand in the United States. Silver Airways is a regional service which offers connections to various destinations in Florida, Pennsylvania, Virginia and West Virginia and provides a service to several islands within the Bahamas. Frontier Airlines is a relatively new budget airline that is mainly focussed on connections around the Rocky Mountain states. Hawaiian Airlines is based in Honolulu and offers connections to the American mainland as well as to Asia. Island Air also serves Hawaii and enjoys a partnership with

SAN DIEGO TRAVEL GUIDE

United Airlines. Mokulele Airlines is a small airline based in Kona Island. It provides access to some of the smaller airports in the Hawaiian Islands. Sun Country Airlines is based in Minneapolis and covers destinations in the United States, Mexico, Costa Rica, Puerto Rica, Jamaica, St Maarten and the US Virgin Islands. Great Lakes Airline is a major participant in the Essential Air Service, a government programme set up to ensure that small and remote communities can be reached by air, following the deregulation of certified airlines. These regional connections include destinations in Arizona, Colorado, Kansas, Minnesota, Nebraska, New Mexico, South Dakota and Wyoming. In the past, Great Lakes Airline had covered a wide range of destinations as a partner under the United Express banner.

Hubs

Hartsfield Jackson Atlanta International Airport serves as the largest hub and headquarters of Delta Airlines. John F. Kennedy International Airport serves as a major hub for Delta's traffic to and from the European continent. Los Angeles International Airport serves as a hub for Delta Airline's connections to Mexico, Hawaii and Japan, but also serves the Florida-California route. Detroit Metropolitan Wayne County Airport is

SAN DIEGO TRAVEL GUIDE

Delta's second largest hubs and serves as a gateway for connections to Asia.

Washington Dulles International Airport serves as a hub for United Airlines as well as Silver Airways. United Airlines also use Denver International Airport, George Bush Intercontinental Airport in Houston, Los Angeles International Airport, San Francisco International Airport, Newark Liberty International Airport and O'Hare International Airport in Chicago as hubs.

Dallas/Fort Worth International Airport serves as the primary hub for American Airlines. Its second largest hub in the southeastern part of the US is Charlotte Douglas International Airport in North Carolina and its largest hub in the north is O'Hare International Airport in Chicago. Other hubs for American Airlines are Phoenix Sky Harbor International Airport - its largest hub in the west - Miami International Airport, Ronald Reagan Washington National Airport, Los Angeles International Airport, John F Kennedy International Airport in New York, which serves as a key hub for European air traffic and La Guardia Airport also in New York.

Seattle-Tacoma International Airport serves as a primary hub for Alaska Airlines. Other hubs for Alaska include Portland International Airport, Los Angeles International Airport and Ted Stevens - Anchorage International Airport. Virgin America

SAN DIEGO TRAVEL GUIDE

operates a primary hub at San Francisco International Airport, but also has a second hub at Los Angeles International Airport as well as a significant presence at Dallas Love Field. Denver International Airport is the primary hub for Frontier Airlines, which also has hubs at Chicago O'Hare International Airport and Orlando International Airport. Frontier also maintains a strong presence at Hartsfield-Jackson Atlanta International Airport, Cincinnati/North Kentucky International Airport, Cleveland Hopkins International Airport, McCarran International Airport in Las Vegas and Philadelphia International Airport. Honolulu International Airport and Kahului Airport serve as hubs for Hawaiian Airlines. Mokulele Airlines uses Kona International Airport and Kahului Airport as hubs. Minneapolis–Saint Paul International Airport serves as a hub for Delta Airlines, Great Lakes Airlines and Sun Country Airlines. Silver Airways uses Fort Lauderdale-Hollywood International Airport as a primary hub and also has hubs at Tampa International Airport, Orlando International Airport and Washington Dulles International Airport.

Seaports

The Port of Miami is often described as the cruise capital of the world, but it also serves as a cargo gateway to the United States. There are 8 passenger terminals and the Port Miami Tunnel, an

SAN DIEGO TRAVEL GUIDE

undersea tunnel connects the port to the Interstate 95 via the Dolphin Expressway. Miami is an important base for several of the world's most prominent cruise lines, including Norwegian Cruise Lines, Celebrity Cruises, Royal Caribbean International and Carnival Cruises. In total, over 40 cruise ships representing 18 different cruise brands are berthed at Miami. Well over 4 million passengers are processed here annually. There are two other important ports in the state of Florida. Port Everglades is the third busiest cruise terminal in Florida, as well as its busiest cargo terminal. It is home to *Allure of the Seas* and *Oasis of the Seas*, two of the world's largest cruise ships. Oceanfront condominium dwellers often bid ships farewell with a friendly cacophony of horns and bells. The third important cruise port in Florida is Port Canaveral, which has 5 cruise terminals.

With its location on the Mississippi river, New Orleans is an important cargo port, but it also has a modern cruise terminal with over 50 check-in counters. The Port of Seattle is operated by the same organization that runs the city's airport. It has two busy cruise terminals. The Port of Los Angeles has a state of the art World Cruise Center, with three berths for passenger liners. As the oldest port on the Gulf of Mexico, the Port of Galveston dates back to the days when Texas was still part of Mexico. Galveston serves both as a cargo port and cruise terminal.

SAN DIEGO TRAVEL GUIDE

🌎 Money Matters

🌎 Currency

The currency of the United States is US dollar (USD). Notes are issued in denominations of $1, $2, $5, $10, $20, $50 and $100. Coins are issued in denominations of $1 (known as a silver dollar, 50c (known as a half dollar), 25c (quarter), 10c (dime), 5c (nickel) and 1c (penny).

🌎 Banking/ATMs

ATM machines are widely distributed across the United States and are compatible with major networks such as Cirrus and Plus for international bank transactions. Most debit cards will display a Visa or MasterCard affiliation, which means that you may be able to use them as a credit card as well. A transaction fee will be charged for withdrawals, but customers of certain bank groups such as Deutsche Bank and Barclays, can be charged smaller transaction fees or none at all, when using the ATM machines of Bank of America. While banking hours will vary, depending on the location and banking group, you can generally expect most banks to be open between 8.30am and 5pm. You will be asked for ID in the form of a passport, when using your debit card for over-the-counter transactions.

While you cannot open a bank account in the United States without a social security number, you may want to consider obtaining a pre-paid debit card, where a fixed amount can be pre-loaded. This service is available from various credit card companies in the United States. The American Express card is called Serve and can be used with a mobile app. You can load more cash at outlets of Walmart, CVS Pharmacy, Dollar General, Family Dollar, Rite Aid and participating 7/Eleven stores.

Credit Cards

Credit cards are widely used in the United States and the the major cards - MasterCard, Visa, American Express and Diners Club – are commonly accepted. A credit card is essential in paying for hotel accommodation or car rental. As a visitor, you may want to check about the fees levied on your card for foreign exchange transactions. While Europe and the UK have already converted to chip-and-pin credit card, the transition is still in progress in the United States. Efforts are being made to make the credit cards of most US stores compliant with chip-and-pin technology. You may find that many stores still employ the older protocols at point-of-sales. Be sure to inform your

SAN DIEGO TRAVEL GUIDE

bank or credit card vendor of your travel plans before leaving home.

🌐 Tourist Tax

In the United States, tourist tax varies from city to city, and can be charged not only on accommodation, but also restaurant bills, car rental and other services that cater mainly to tourists. In 22 states, some form of state wide tax is charged for accommodation and 38 states levy a tax on car rental. The city that levies the highest tax bill is Chicago. Apart from a flat fee of $2.75, you can expect to be charged 16 percent per day on hotel accommodation as well as nearly 25% for car rentals. New York charges an 18 percent hotel tax, as does Nashville, while Kansas City, Houston and Indianapolis levy around 17 percent per day hotel tax. Expect to pay 16.5 percent tax per day on your hotel bill in Cleveland and 15.6 percent per day in Seattle, with a 2 percent hike, if staying in the Seattle Tourism Improvement Area. Las Vegas charges 12 percent hotel tax. In Los Angeles, you will be charged a whopping 14 percent on your hotel room, but in Burbank, California, the rate is only 2 percent. Dallas, Texas only charges 2 percent on hotels with more than a hundred rooms. In Portland a city tax of 6 percent is added to a county tax of 5.5 percent. Do inquire about the hotel tax rate in the city where you intend to stay, when booking your accommodation.

🌐 Sales Tax

In the United States, the sales tax rate is set at state level, but in most states local counties can set an additional surtax. In some states, groceries and/or prescription drugs will be exempt from tax or charged at a lower rate. There are only five states that charge no state sales tax at all. They are Oregon, Delaware, New Hampshire, Alaska and Montana. Alaska allows a local tax rate not exceeding 7 percent and in Montana, local authorities are enabled to set a surtax rate, should they wish to do so. The state sales tax is generally set at between 4 percent (Alabama, Georgia, Louisiana, and Wyoming) and 7 percent (Indiana, Mississippi, New Jersey, Tennessee, Rhode Island) although there are exceptions outside that spectrum with Colorado at 2.8 percent and California at 7.5 percent. The local surcharge can be anything from 4.7 percent (Hawaii) to around 11 percent (Oklahoma and Louisiana). Can you claim back tax on your US purchases as a tourist? In the United States, sales tax is added retro-actively upon payment, which means that it will not be included in the marked price of the goods you buy. Because it is set at state, rather than federal level, it is usually not refundable.

Two states do offer sales tax refunds to tourists. In Texas you will be able to get tax back from over 6000 participating stores if the tax amount came to more than $12 and the goods were purchased within 30 days of your departure. To qualify, you need to submit the original sales receipts, your passport, flight or transport information and visa details. Refunds are made in cash, cheque or via PayPal. Louisiana was the first state to introduce tax refunds for tourists. To qualify there, you must submit all sales receipts, together with your passport and flight ticket at a Refund Center outlet.

Tipping

Tipping is very common in the United States. In sit-down restaurants, a tip of between 10 and 15 percent of the bill is customary. At many restaurants, the salaries of waiting staff will be well below minimum wage levels. With large groups of diners, the restaurant may charge a mandatory gratuity, which is automatically included in the bill. At the trendiest New York restaurants, a tip of 25 percent may be expected. While you can add a credit card tip, the best way to ensure the gratuity reaches your server is to tip separately in cash. Although tipping is less of an obligation at takeaway restaurants, such as McDonalds, you can leave your change, or otherwise $1, if there is a tip jar on the counter. In the case of pizza delivery, a minimum of $3 is recommended and more is obviously appreciated. Although a delivery charge is often levied, this money usually goes to the pizzeria, rather than the driver. Tip a taxi driver 10 percent of the total fare. At your hotel, tip the porter between $1 and $2 per bag. Tip between 10 and 20 percent at hair salons, spas, beauty salons and barber shops. Tip tour guides between 10 and 20 percent for a short excursion. For a day trip, tip both the guide and the driver $5 to $10 per person, if a gratuity is not included in the cost of the tour. Tip the drivers of charter or sightseeing buses around $1 per person.

Connectivity

Mobile Phones

There are four major service providers for wireless connection in the United States. They are Verizon Wireless, T-Mobile US, AT&T Mobility and Sprint. Not all are compatible with European standards. While most countries in Europe, Asia, the Middle East and East Africa uses the GSM mobile network, only two US service providers, T-Mobile and AT&T Mobility aligns with this. Also bear in mind that GSM carriers in the United States operate using the 850 MHz/1900 MHz frequency

SAN DIEGO TRAVEL GUIDE

bands, whereas the UK, all of Europe, Asia, Australia and Africa use 900/1800MHz. You should check with your phone's tech specifications to find out whether it supports these standards. The other services, Verizon Wireless and Sprint use the CDMA network standard and, while Verizon's LTE frequencies are somewhat compatible with those of T-Mobile and AT&T, Sprint uses a different bandwidth for its LTE coverage.

To use your own phone, you can purchase a T-Mobile 3-in-1 starter kit for $20. If your device is unlocked, GMS-capable and supports either Band II (1900 MHz) or Band IV (1700/2100 MHz), you will be able to access the T-Mobile network. You can also purchase an AT&T sim card through the Go Phone Pay-as-you-go plan for as little as $0.99. Refill cards are available from $25 and are valid for 90 days. If you want to widen your network options, you may want to explore the market for a throwaway or disposable phone. At Walmart, you can buy non-contracted phones for as little as $9.99, as well as pre-paid sim cards and data top-up packages.

Canadians travellers will find the switch to US networks technically effortless, but should watch out for roaming costs. Several American networks do offer special international rates for calls to Canada or Mexico.

SAN DIEGO TRAVEL GUIDE

Dialing Code

The international dialing code for the United States is +1.

Emergency Numbers

General Emergency: 911 (this number can be used free of charge from any public phone in the United States).
MasterCard: 1-800-307-7309
Visa: 1-800-847-2911

General Information

Public Holidays

1 January: New Year's Day
3rd Monday in January: Martin Luther King Day
3rd Monday in February: President's Day
Last Monday in May: Memorial Day
4 July: Independence Day
1st Monday in September: Labour Day
2nd Monday in October: Columbus Day
11 November: Veteran's Day
4th Thursday in November: Thanksgiving Day

SAN DIEGO TRAVEL GUIDE

4th Friday in November: Day after Thanksgiving

25 December: Christmas Day (if Christmas Day falls on a Sunday, the Monday thereafter is a public holiday.) In some states, 26 December is a public holiday as well.

There are several festivals that are not public holidays per se, but are culturally observed in the United States. They include:

14 February: Valentine's Day

17 March: St Patrick's Day

March/April (variable): Easter or Passover

Second Sunday in May: Mother's Day

3rd Sunday in June: Father's Day

31 October: Halloween

Time Zones

The United States has 6 different time zones. **Eastern Standard Time** is observed in the states of Maine, New York, New Hampshire, Delaware, Vermont, Maryland, Rhode Island, Massachusetts, Connecticut, Pennsylvania, Ohio, North Carolina, South Carolina, Georgia, Virginia, West Virginia, Michigan, most of Florida and Indiana as well as the eastern parts of Kentucky and Tennessee. Eastern Standard Time is calculated as Greenwich Meantime/Coordinated Universal Time (UTC) -5. **Central Standard Time** is observed in Iowa, Illinois, Missouri, Arkansas, Louisiana, Oklahoma, Kansas,

SAN DIEGO TRAVEL GUIDE

Mississippi, Alabama, near all of Texas, the western half of Kentucky, the central and western part of Tennessee, sections of the north-western and south-western part of Indiana, most of North and South Dakota, the eastern and central part of Nebraska and the north-western strip of Florida, also known as the Florida Panhandle. Central Standard Time is calculated as Greenwich Meantime/Coordinated Universal Time (UTC) -6. **Mountain Standard Time** is observed in New Mexico, Colorado, Wyoming, Montana, Utah, Arizona, the southern and central section of Idaho, the western parts of Nebraska, South Dakota and North Dakota, a portion of eastern Oregon and the counties of El Paso and Hudspeth in Texas. Mountain Standard Time is calculated as Greenwich Meantime/Coordinated Universal Time (UTC) -7. **Pacific Standard Time** is used in California, Washington, Nevada, most of Oregon and the northern part of Idaho. Pacific Standard Time is calculated as Greenwich Meantime/Coordinated Universal Time (UTC) -8. **Alaska Standard Time** is used in Alaska and this can be calculated as Greenwich Meantime/Coordinated Universal Time (UTC) -9. Because of its distant location, Hawaii is in a time zone of its own. **Hawaii Standard Time** can be calculated as Greenwich Meantime/Coordinated Universal Time (UTC) -10.

SAN DIEGO TRAVEL GUIDE

🌐 Daylight Savings Time

Clocks are set forward one hour at 2.00am on the second Sunday of March and set back one hour at 2.00am on the first Sunday of November for Daylight Savings Time. The states of Hawaii and Arizona do not observe Daylight Savings Time. However, the Navajo Indian Reservation, which extends across three states (Arizona, Utah and New Mexico), does observe Daylight Savings Time throughout its lands, including that portion which falls within Arizona.

🌐 School Holidays

In the United States, the academic year begins in September, usually in the week just before or after Labour Day and ends in the early or middle part of June. There is a Winter Break that includes Christmas and New Year and a Spring Break in March or April that coincides with Easter. In some states, there is also a Winter Break in February. The summer break occurs in the 10 to 11 weeks between the ending of one academic year and the commencement of the next academic year. Holidays may vary according to state and certain weather conditions such as hurricanes or snowfall may also lead to temporary school closures in affected areas.

SAN DIEGO TRAVEL GUIDE

🌐 Trading Hours

Trading hours in the United States vary. Large superstores like Walmart trade round the clock at many of its outlets, or else between 7am and 10pm. Kmart is often open from 8am to 10pm, 7 days a week. Target generally opens at 8am and may close at 10 or 11pm, depending on the area. Many malls will open at 10am and close at 9pm. Expect restaurants to be open from about 11am to 10pm or 11pm, although the hours of eateries that serve alcohol and bars may be restricted by local legislation. Banking hours also vary, according to branch and area. Branches of the Bank of America will generally open at 9am, and closing time can be anywhere between 4pm and 6pm. Most post office outlets are open from 9am to 5pm on weekdays.

🌐 Driving

In the United States, motorists drive on the right hand side of the road. As public transport options are not always adequate, having access to a car is virtually essential, when visiting the United States. To drive, you will need a valid driver's licence from your own country, in addition to an international driving permit. If your driver's licence does not include a photograph,

SAN DIEGO TRAVEL GUIDE

you will be asked to submit your passport for identification as well.

For car rental, you will also need a credit card. Some companies do not rent out vehicles to drivers under the age of 25. Visitors with a UK license may need to obtain a check code for rental companies, should they wish to verify the details and validity of their driver's licence, via the DVLA view-your-licence service. This can also be generated online, but must be done at least 72 hours prior to renting the car. In most cases, though, the photo card type license will be enough. The largest rental companies - Alamo, Avis, Budget, Hertz, Dollar and Thrifty - are well represented in most major cities and usually have offices at international airports. Do check about the extent of cover included in your travel insurance package and credit card agreement. Some credit card companies may include Collision Damage Waiver (CDW), which will cover you against being held accountable for any damage to the rental car, but it is recommended that you also arrange for personal accident insurance, out-of-state insurance and supplementary liability insurance. You can sometimes cut costs on car rentals by reserving a car via the internet before leaving home.

The maximum speed limit in the United States varies according to state, but is usually between 100km per hour (65 m.p.h.) and 120km per hour (75 m.p.h.). For most of the Eastern states, as well as California and Oregon on the west coast the maximum speed driven on interstate highways should be 110km per hour (70 m.p.h.). Urban speed legislation varies, but in business and residential areas, speeds are usually set between 32km (20 miles) and 48km (30 miles) per hour. In Colorado, nighttime speed limits apply in certain areas where migrating wildlife could be endangered and on narrow, winding mountain passes, a limit of 32km (20 miles) per hour sometimes applies. In most American states there is a ban on texting for all drivers and a ban on all cell phone use for novice drivers.

Drinking

It is illegal in all 50 states for persons under the age of 21 to purchase alcohol or to be intoxicated. In certain states, such as Texas, persons between the age of 18 and 21 may be allowed to drink beer or wine, if in the company of a parent or legal guardian. In most states, the trading hours for establishments selling alcohol is limited. There are a few exceptions to this. In Nevada, alcohol may be sold round the clock and with few restrictions other than age. In Louisiana, there are no restrictions on trading in alcohol at state level, although some counties set their own restrictions. By contrast, Arizona has some of the strictest laws in relation to alcohol sales, consumption and driving under the influence. The sale of alcohol is prohibited on Native American reservations, unless

SAN DIEGO TRAVEL GUIDE

the tribal council of that reservation has passed a vote to lift restrictions.

Smoking

There is no smoking ban set at federal level in the United States. At state level, there are 40 states in total that enact some form of state wide restriction on smoking, although the exemptions of individual states may vary. In Arizona, California, Colorado, Connecticut, Delaware, Hawaii, Illinois, Iowa, Kansas, Maine, Maryland, Massachusetts, Michigan, Minnesota, Montana, Nebraska, North Dakota, New Jersey, New Mexico, New York, Ohio, Oregon, Rhode Island, South Dakota, Utah, Vermont, Washington and Wisconsin, smoking is prohibited in all public enclosed areas, including bars and restaurants. The states of Arkansas, Florida, Indiana, Louisiana, Pennsylvania and Tennessee do have a general state wide restriction on smoking in public places, but exempt adult venues where under 21s are not allowed. This includes bars, restaurants, betting shops and gaming parlours (Indiana) and casinos (Louisiana and Pennsylvania). Nevada also has a state wide ban on smoking that exempts casinos, bars, strip clubs and brothels. In Georgia, state wide smoking legislation exempts bars and restaurants that only serve patrons over the age of 18. Idaho has a state wide ban that includes restaurants, but exempts bars serving only alcohol. New Hampshire, North Carolina and Virginia have also introduced some form of state wide smoking restriction. While the states of Alabama, Alaska, Kentucky, Mississippi, Missouri, Oklahoma, South Carolina, Texas, West Virginia and Wyoming have no state legislation, there are more specific restrictions at city and county level. In Arizona, there is an exemption for businesses located on Native American reservation and, in particular, for Native American religious ceremonies that may include smoking rituals. In California, the first state to implement anti-smoking legislation, smoking is also prohibited in parks and on sidewalks.

Electricity

Electricity: 110 volts

Frequency: 60 Hz

Electricity sockets are compatible with American Type A and Type B plugs. The Type A plug features two flat prongs or blades, while the Type B plug has the same plus an additional 'earth' prong. Most newer models of camcorders and cameras are dual voltage, which means that you should be able to charge them without an adapter in the United States, as they have a built in converter for voltage. You may find that appliances from the UK or Europe which were designed to accommodate a higher voltage will not function as effectively in the United

SAN DIEGO TRAVEL GUIDE

States. While a current converter or transformer will be able to adjust the voltage, you may still experience some difficulty with the type of devices that are sensitive to variations in frequency as the United States uses 60 Hz, instead of the 50 Hz which is common in Europe and the UK. Appliances like hairdryers will usually be available in hotels and since electronic goods are fairly cheap in the United States, the easiest strategy may be to simply purchase a replacement. Bear in mind, that you may need an adaptor or transformer to operate it once you return home.

🌏 Food & Drink

Hamburgers, hot dogs and apple pie may be food items that come to mind when considering US culinary stereotypes, but Americans eat a wide variety of foods. They love steaks and ribs when dining out and pancakes or waffles for breakfast. As a society which embraces various immigrant communities, America excels at adopting and adapting traditional staples and adding its own touch to them. Several "Asian" favorites really originated in the United States. These include the California roll (offered in sushi restaurants) and the fortune cookie (chinese). Popular Hispanic imports include tacos, enchiladas and burritos. Another stereotype of American cuisine is large portion sizes. Hence the existence of American inventions such as the

SAN DIEGO TRAVEL GUIDE

footlong sub, the footlong chilli cheese hot dog and the Krispy Creme burger, which combines a regular hamburger with a donut. Corn dogs are fairground favorites. Most menus are more balanced however. It is common to ask for a doggy bag (to take away remaining food) in a restaurant.

When in the South, enjoy corn bread, grits and southern fried chicken. Try spicy buffalo wings in New York, traditionally prepared baked beans in Boston and deep dish pizza in Chicago. French fries are favorites with kids of all ages, but Americans also love their potatoes as hash browns or the bite sized tater tots. Indulge your sweet tooth with Twinkies, pop tarts, cup cakes and banana splits. Popular sandwiches include the BLT (bacon, lettuce, tomato, the Reuben sandwich, the sloppy joe and the peanut butter and jelly.

Sodas (fizzy drinks) and bottled waters are the top beverages in the United States. The top selling soft drinks are Coca Cola, followed by Pepsi Cola, Diet Coke, Mountain Dew and Dr Pepper. In America's colonial past, tea was initially the hot beverage of choice and it was tea politics that kicked off the American Revolution, but gradually tea has been replaced by coffee in popularity. From the 1970s, Starbucks popularized coffee culture in the United States. Americans still drink gallons of tea and they are particularly fond of a refreshing glass of iced tea. Generally, Americans drink more beer than wine and favorite brands include Bud Light, followed by Coors Light, Budweiser and Miller Light. Popular cocktails are the Martini, the Manhattan, the Margarita, the Bloody Mary, the Long Island Ice tea and Sex on the Beach.

American Sports

Baseball is widely regarded as the national sport of America. The sport originated in the mid 1800s and superficially shares the basic objective of cricket, which is to score runs by hitting a ball pitched by the opposing team, but in baseball, the innings ends as soon as three players have been caught out. A point is scored when a runner has passed three bases and reached the 4th or home base of the baseball diamond. After 9 innings, the team with the highest number of runs is declared the winner. The Baseball World Series is played in the fall (autumn), usually in October, and consists of best-of-seven play-off between the two top teams representing the rival affiliations of the National League and American League.

Although the origins of American football can be found in rugby, the sport is now widely differentiated from its roots and today numerous distinctions exist between the two. In American football, a game is divided into four quarters, with each team fielding 11 players, although unlimited substitution is allowed.

SAN DIEGO TRAVEL GUIDE

Players wear helmets and heavy padding as any player can be tackled, regardless of ball possession. An annual highlight is the Super Bowl, the championship game of the National Football League. The event is televised live to over a 100 million viewers and features a high profile halftime performance by a top music act. Super bowl Sunday traditionally takes place on the first Sunday of February.

The roots of stock car racing can be found in America's prohibition era, when bootleggers needed powerful muscle cars (often with modifications for greater speed) to transport their illicit alcohol stocks. Informal racing evolved to a lively racing scene in Daytona, Florida. An official body, NASCAR, was founded in 1948 to regulate the sport, NASCAR. Today, NASCAR racing has millions of fans. One of its most prestigious events is the Sprint Cup, a championship which comprises of 36 races and kicks off each year with the Daytona 500.

Rodeo originated from the chores and day-to-day activities of Spanish cattle farmers and later, the American ranchers who occupied the former Spanish states such as Texas, California and Arizona. The advent of fencing eliminated the need for cattle drives, but former cowboys found that their skills still offered good entertainment, providing a basis for wild west shows such as those presented by Buffalo Bill. Soon, rodeo events became the highlight of frontier towns throughout the west. During the first half of the 20th centuries, organizations formed to regulate events. Today, rodeo is considered a legitimate national sport with millions of fans. If you want to experience the thrill of this extreme sport, attend one of its top events. The Prescott Frontier Days show in Arizona is billed to be America's oldest rodeo. The Reno Rodeo in Nevada is a 10 day event that takes place in mid-June and includes the option of closer participation as a volunteer. Rodeo Houston, a large 20 day event that takes place towards the end of winter, is coupled to a livestock show. Visit the San Antonio show in Texas during February for the sheer variety of events. The National Western Rodeo in Denver Colorado is an indoor event that attracts up to half a million spectators each year. The National Finals that takes place in Las Vegas during December is the prestigious championship that marks the end of the year's rodeo calendar.

Useful Websites

https://esta.cbp.dhs.gov/esta/ -- The US Electronic System for Travel Authorization
http://www.visittheusa.com/
http://roadtripusa.com/
http://www.roadtripamerica.com/

SAN DIEGO TRAVEL GUIDE

http://www.road-trip-usa.info/

http://www.autotoursusa.com/

http://www.onlyinyourstate.com/

http://www.theamericanroadtripcompany.co.uk/

Printed in Great Britain
by Amazon